IMPROVING YOUR CRAFT FOR THE PROFESSIONAL WRITER

Business for Breakfast: Volume 18

LEAH CUTTER

Knotted Road Press

Improving Your Craft for the Professional Writer
Business for Breakfast: Volume 18
Copyright © 2022 Leah Cutter
All rights reserved
Published by Knotted Road Press
www.KnottedRoadPress.com

ISBN: 978-1-64470-269-7

Cover and interior design copyright © 2022 Knotted Road Press
http://www.KnottedRoadPress.com

Reviews
It's true. Reviews help me sell more books. If you've enjoyed this story, please consider leaving a review of it on your favorite site.

Come someplace new…
Are you a traveler? Do you enjoy exploring strange new worlds, new cultures, new people?

Journey into the various lands envisioned by Leah R Cutter.

Sign up for my newsletter and I'll start you on your travels with a free copy of my book, *The Island Sampler*.

http://www.LeahCutter.com/newsletter/

All rights reserved. Except for brief quotations in critical articles or reviews, the purchaser or reader may not modify, copy, distribute, transmit, display perform, reproduce, publish, license, create derivative works from, transfer or sell any information contained in this book without the express written permission of Leah Cutter or Knotted Road Press. Requests to use or quote this material for any purpose should be addressed to Knotted Road Press.

Disclaimer
This book is provided for general educational purposes. While the author has used her best efforts in preparing this book, Knotted Road Press makes no representation with respect to the accuracy or completeness of the contents, or about the suitability of the information contained herein for any purpose. All content is provided "as is" without warranty of any kind.

Also by Leah Cutter

Urban/Contemporary Fantasy Series

The Witch's Progress

Circle of Air
Circle of Fire
Circle of Water
Circle of Earth

Seattle Trolls

The Changeling Troll
The Princess Troll
The Fairy-Bridge Troll
The Troll-Demon War
The Troll-Human War
The Troll-Troll War

The Cassie Stories

Poisoned Pearls
Tainted Waters
Spoiled Harvest
Bloodied Ice

The Shadow Wars Trilogy

The Raven and the Dancing Tiger

The Guardian Hound

War Among the Crocodiles

The Clockwork Fairy Kingdom

The Clockwork Fairy Kingdom

The Maker, the Teacher, and the Monster

The Dwarven Wars

The Chronicles of Franklin

Franklin Versus The Popcorn Thief

Franklin Versus The Soul Thief

Franklin Versus The Child Thief

Epic Fantasy Series

Houses of the Dead

Houses Divided

Houses Fallen

Houses Reborn

Forgotten Gods

A Wind Blown Torment

A Stone Strewn Clash

A Sea Washed Victory

The Tanesh Empire Trilogy

The Glass Magician

The Desert Heart

The Ghost Dog

Huli Intergalactic: Science/Space Fantasy

Origins

The Strawberry Girl

Mysteries

The Purloined Letter Opener

Dancer in Darkness

Trophy Hunters

The Alvin Goodfellow Case Files

The Rabbit Mysteries

The Shredded Veil Mysteries

Mystery, Crime, and Mayhem

Contents

Introduction	xi
1. Becoming a Confident Gardener	1
2. Writing a Clean First Draft	5
3. Ignoring Critical Voice	11
4. Learning to Listen to Creative Voice	17
5. The Giggle Test (Writing is Hard!)	23
6. Ideas are Cheap	29
7. Gaining Speed	33
8. Beyond Book One	39
9. No Secret Handshake	43
Afterword	47
About the Author	49
About Knotted Road Press	51

For Sonia, who inspired me to write this book

Introduction

I talk writing with friends frequently. I mean, what else do you do when you get a bunch of writers together but talk craft and business? Anyway—some of them always seem to be amazed at how far along the path in terms of writing craft and process that I seem to be.

However, I want to assure y'all that I didn't spring forth from the brow of Zeus fully formed. I started off in the 1990s (and beyond) completely ensconced in the myths that *writing is rewriting*, that of course it took a full year to write a novel, and that by insisting that I get *paid* for my work was somehow cheapening it.

I sold my first novel back in 2001, when the only real path to publication was through traditional publishers. I worked with a New York publisher for my first three novels.

Then, my life imploded. I stopped writing. I still did art—I painted watercolors and I quilted. But there weren't many words.

Finally, after two years, I decided to get back to the writing. An idea grabbed me and just wouldn't let go. So I took three years (because it took at least a year to write a novel, don't you know) to write an unsellable trilogy.

Introduction

By the time I finished it, the world had changed. Indie publishing had started and was becoming a thing.

I wouldn't say that I jumped in with both feet, because it took me a while to warm to the notion.

However, before I did that, I was lucky enough to shed a lot of the traditional publishing myths so I *could* move forward. This journey started when I ran into Dean Wesley Smith's series on *Killing the Sacred Cows of Publishing*.

I was pointed to his site by other writers on a professional writer forum. They were making fun of what Dean was saying.

Me, not feeling comfortable with what the other writers were saying, went to Dean's site to see the original source material.

I read through the myths that he was exposing. And I got really, *really* mad at myself for believing in them. (The chapter on agents was particularly damning. I mean, why exactly was I taking *legal* advice on a *legal* document from someone who didn't practice law?)

That was when I started to catch a clue that my methods in terms of writing and craft weren't necessarily the way that all writers worked. That there was a different way, a different path, and that maybe that path would work for me.

So this is that journey, working on improving my craft, from the starting point of being a traditionally published author to now being an independent publishing powerhouse.

Though the steps of your individual journey will be different, I hope the signposts that I'm putting up will help you along the way.

Are you ready?

Let's go.

Leah Cutter
Ravensdale, WA

ONE

Becoming a Confident Gardener

So much of writing and craft is intertwined together. I am going to tease apart the elements that I can. However, I may send you back and forth between the chapters in this book, because the terminology and concepts are the same.

One of the concepts that I'll use more than once in this book is the distinction between *architect* and *gardener*, when it comes to writing.

An *architect* plans out their writing beforehand. It may just be a back of the napkin quick sketch. It may be full blown blueprints. It is what works for them.

A *gardener*, on the other hand, doesn't do that level of formal planning when it comes to plotting out a story. They may do a lot of world building ahead of time, fleshing out characters, worlds, currencies, socio-political patterns, technology, and so on. But they still might not have a clue where the story is going to go, or what's going to happen. Instead, they race along, madly scattering seeds, then harvesting the bits that grow and are interesting.

I have never been a full-fledged architect. Even at the start. Instead, I called myself a *gestalt* writer. I would get pieces of a novel—the start, a few scenes in the middle, and a general sense of the end—but not the entire thing. It always felt like a brilliant flash when it happened. Then I would be able to write the thing, pulling in those pieces as necessary.

In terms of writing short stories, when I was first taking writing fairly seriously, so in my thirties, I couldn't finish a story if I didn't know where the ending was going to be. I had many (many!) short stories that I started and never finished, because at that point, I needed that clear trail ahead of me.

However, at the same time, I always had to be careful about how much of a story I plotted out. If I told myself too much of what was going to happen, I couldn't finish the story either. I'd get bored, because in my head, I'd already told the story. Why should I bother repeating that exercise by writing it all out?

Around novel six, I started a novel without the *gestalt* feeling first. Just sat down and started writing. I was inspired by Dean to do so. I had no idea if I'd succeed or not. But I wanted to try.

It was an amazing experience. Exhilarating. Frightening. I started describing it as jumping off a cliff and trusting that my wings would form as I was sailing down.

I *loved* that feeling.

As I wrote that book, (the first of the Clockwork Fairy Kingdom trilogy) I found I was getting glimpses of what was ahead, maybe one or two chapters or so, not a lot. I had no idea where or what the ending was. It didn't matter. The writing grew easier as I went along, trusting myself, trusting the process. I found the ending, and it was completely satisfying to me (and to my readers—it's still a novel that I get fan mail for).

That novel was when I discovered I was truly a gardener. I loved making shit up when I hit the page. There was no stopping me at that point. Pretty much every time I sat down, I would hit that white hot flow of creation.

I finished novel number fifty-five last year. I am quite

confident in my ability to tell a story. For the most part, I can now start a short story with no idea of where the ending is, and just write until it's finished. There are still times, though, when I have the entire story plotted out before I start writing it.

As for novels, there are times now when I plot things out. But my notes are never extensive. The longest "outline" I've done for a novel was 1200 words, where I wrote out a sentence for each chapter. The shortest was thirty-six words. I needed to plot out the emotional arc of the two POV characters. While each character was doing completely different things, their emotional state was almost identical for every chapter, so just a few words on the state of their emotions, nothing about what they were doing.

I have become a confident gardener, trusting in my ability to write a novel without any idea of where I'm going. I can even now write entire series with only the vaguest clue of where I'm going to end up.

How did I get there?

I've thought about that a lot, trying to come up with guidance. However, as far as I can figure out, the way I arrived at this stage was by writing. A lot. One novel after another, one short story after another.

I know that isn't the answer you wanted to hear. You are (possibly) reading this book in search of the secret handshake. I have an entire chapter on that later. (LINK) But—spoiler alert!—there is no secret handshake. No fast and easy way to suddenly make yourself success. No "skip the line" method for being a better artist.

You need to put in the work. You need to figure out your process for writing. Then you need to do it.

Writing is supposed to be fun. I'll talk more about that later. (LINK) However, for now, if you suspect that you are any sort of gardener, and you want to be more confident in your gardening, as it were, my best advice for you is to get out there and do it. The more you practice, the better you'll be at it.

Not every chapter is going to have this as a moral. I just wanted to start out with this, to get the disappointment out of the way. Learn to trust the process. Learn to trust yourself.

You won't be sorry when you do.

In Conclusion:

- *Architects* plan out their writing in advance. *Gardeners* don't.
- Writing is supposed to be fun. If you find that it isn't, perhaps you need to look at your style. Try being a gardener for a while if you've never done that before.
- The best way to learn your style, and to become confident writing that way, is to write. A lot. Then write some more.

TWO

Writing a Clean First Draft

As I said before, I was fully immersed in the myths about how *writing is rewriting* and how you couldn't possibly write a clean first draft.

However, I *hated* editing. Or rewriting. It was the absolute worst thing in the world to me. I despised every soul-sucking moment of it.

Yet, I was willing to put up with it if that was what it took to be a writer.

I could write a novel in six months. (Honestly, that was all it took for my first novel.) By the time I wrote my sixth novel, I was able to write a novel in about six weeks. Then I would take *forever* to do the rewriting, because I hated it so much. That novel that took six weeks to write? Took twelve weeks to edit. Possibly more.

My process, from my first novel up until my eighth or nineth, was to write out everything twice. I would hand-write the first draft. I had a collection of beautiful fountain pens that I collected over the years that I used for all my novels.

While I used expensive pens, I wrote on cheap paper. Just yellow legal pads. I found that if I tried writing in expensive, fancy notebooks, I wouldn't write anything at all, because it wasn't going to be perfect, or even good. The cheap paper allowed me to just scribble down anything I wanted and it would be fine if I wasted the paper.

I would write a chapter or so out by hand, then I'd type that into the computer. I'd fix a *lot* of things in that typed draft, but not everything. No, I kept a spreadsheet to the side, where I noted things that still needed to be fixed in previous chapters, instead of going in and actually fixing those things as I went along.

I'd hand-write the next chapter, as if those things that I'd noted had already been fixed, which led occasionally to continuity errors, as when I went back to fix something I'd change something else. (*Sigh.*) It was a nightmare of constant rewriting and editing when it came to that phase.

Then I came across the concept that my rewriting was actually *hurting* my writing.

You see, you started learning story from the time you were born. Possibly earlier, if your parents read to you when you were in the womb.

Every day, you consume story. From listening to your friends. From reading or watching some sort of media. Many commercials and ads tell stories. And you told your own stories.

By the time you're reading this, you have a bone-deep understanding of how story works in your culture. Possibly how it works in other cultures as well, depending on where you grew up.

However, you didn't start critiquing stories until you went to school. Didn't learn to question a narrative or deconstruct a point of view possibly until you were in your teens.

And while you continue to practice story every single day of your life, chances are, you do *not* practice doing critiques every day. In fact, you might have stopped doing that once you left school.

This means that your storytelling abilities far surpass your critiquing abilities. When you rewrite a story, your critique of the story will actually bring down the level of quality of your story, not elevate it.

Here's a picture that shows what happens when you rewrite a story.

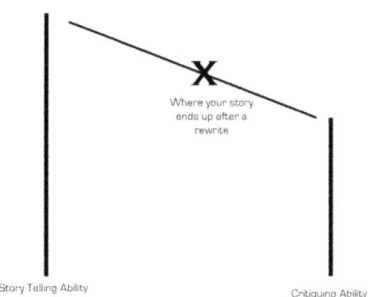

Your storytelling ability is high. Your critiquing ability—not so much. Rewriting the story brings down the level of quality.

Learning about this was a complete gamechanger for me.

I didn't *have* to rewrite! I already knew how to tell a story!

What I had to do, though, was to figure out how to clear out all the crap and write a clean first draft.

Let me assure you, even though this was my stated goal, I was *not* able to automatically start writing clean first drafts. It took me two years, maybe three or four novels and numerous short stories, before I taught myself how to do it.

Which I figure is encouraging, right? If I could teach myself to do it, you can as well!

I kept the same process I had in terms of generating new words, that is, writing everything out by hand then typing it in. However, instead of keeping a spreadsheet with everything that needed to be fixed, I went in and fixed things when I came across them.

I became "unstuck" in terms of my novel. I no longer had

to experience it as a reader experienced it. I could go back and forth at will.

Next, I would start finish typing up a chapter, then just continue typing up the next chapter, instead of going back to handwriting. Eventually, I'd get stuck, and I'd have to go write out the rest of the chapter by hand. It was a back and forth process.

Eventually, I started a novel on the computer, and finished it there as well. I wrote a (mostly) clean draft. It took me twenty days.

Part of my issue, at least at the start, was that I was still writing "thin" first drafts. I would have my first readers go through the draft, and I'd end up adding another 20-30% to the final draft. That took longer to fix, but eventually, I figured out how to slow down enough to add in all the things that needed adding as I was writing it.

Plus, I added another technique: cycling.

Cycling is basically going back over what you've already written. The difference between cycling and rewriting is that with cycling, you're still in creative voice, not critical voice. I will get into cycling a lot more in a later chapter. LINK

In the meanwhile, you get to start thinking about how you can change your process so that you write a clean first draft. It is possible to do. It will make you a faster and better writer, because those words will still have all the heart and soul in them that you, as an artist, intended.

NOTE: The idea of a clean first draft may fill you with dread. It may frighten you. This is perfectly normal, because you're thinking about exposing yourself to the world. It means letting your inner artist out to play. This is all scary stuff. However, for most people, being a better artist means allowing that artist room to breathe.

There is a singular group of people for whom writing a clean first draft is impossible. Those are the people whose inner, critical voice is so harsh and demanding that trying to write something cleanly means they write nothing at all. I know more people who've managed to train their critical voice to shut up, but there are a few writers I know who cannot manage it, though they've tried for years.

For them, writing a messy first draft gives them permission to write. They cannot get any words on the page unless it's messy. These types of writers are actually very few. Most writers can get beyond that.

So while most of you will be able to write a clean first draft after you train yourself to do it, I will acknowledge that there are going to be a few of you who will never manage that. You're just going to have to learn other techniques for managing your critical voice, the one that stops you from writing as well as from doing your best work.

In Conclusion:

- You don't have to rewrite in order to produce good work.
- It may take time to train yourself to write a clean first draft. That's okay. For me, that work was well worth it.
- Writing a clean first draft may scare you. Try doing it anyway.
- You may be one of the **VERY** few who can't write a clean first draft. Try anyway, then try again, and try again, until you're absolutely certain that you can't. However, most people can learn this technique.

THREE

Ignoring Critical Voice

WHILE YOU MAY HAVE many voices competing in your head, there are two primary ones: critical voice and creative voice.

Think of your critical voice as the voice of your parent, or your English teacher, or whoever it was who criticized you when you were younger.

On the one hand, your critical voice is trying to keep you safe. It's the voice of "reason," of society at large, that group that's trying to get you to follow the rules.

Whereas your creative voice is the child who just wants to play. I've often described my creative voice as the two year old who wants to take off all her clothes, go run out into the street, and play in traffic.

Critical voice is the one who says *no*. Put on your clothes. Don't talk to strangers. Don't lick that! Don't ask questions. Don't *stare*. You must at least pretend to know what you're talking about. You must follow these rules of grammar. You will be laughed at if you write that. Your family is going to disown you if you bring up that topic.

And so on. I'm sure that you can add your own critical voice lines to this.

As I said before, critical voice is here to keep you safe.

Art is not supposed to be safe.

I'm going to repeat that.

Art is not supposed to be safe.

This is why critical voice can stop you in your tracks and prevent you from even trying. Why should I bother writing this? No one will read it. It won't sell.

That's all critical voice, trying to prevent you from exposing yourself.

You know how to tell a story. Critical voice is the one that says your story isn't good enough.

Usually, unless you've done a lot of work, critical voice is also the one in charge of rewriting. This means that even if you aren't intending it to, critical voice will strip the emotion and soul out of a piece in an effort to protect you. It may be a very pretty piece by the time you've finished rewriting it, with beautiful words, but the heart and soul will be missing.

And readers read to feel something. Particularly readers of genre fiction. If all you care about is pretty words, you shouldn't be reading this book. I'm a commercial artist, advising people on commercial art. Not literature. Which actually doesn't sell.

So how do you learn to ignore critical voice?

Before I stopped rewriting, I discovered that my critical voice wasn't very active in the mornings. I would get up, not even shower, but go straight from my bed to my writing (trailing clouds of dreams behind me). My inner editor was still fast asleep, and I'd get my best writing done really early. I was still handwriting everything at the time. I'd type up what I'd written in the afternoons/evenings, when my editor was more awake. At that point, I found it useful to have a more critical eye, to add in the details I was missing.

Once I started writing everything out in a single draft, straight onto the computer, I found it much more difficult to shut critical voice up. I'd be typing away and I'd suddenly find myself staring at the refrigerator. (Anyone who works from home will tell you that the fridge is the most dangerous appliance in your home. You'll often just find yourself in front of it, staring.)

I wouldn't remember necessarily leaving the keyboard. I'd just find myself someplace else.

I'd have to spend time, then, reconstructing what had just occurred, why I was no longer writing. Generally, it was fear. I'd run across something that woke critical voice up and I was suddenly afraid to continue. It was usually one of the fears above, that people will hate you for writing this, your family will disown you, you haven't done enough research yet to write about this, and so on.

Once I figured out what was bothering me, my response was to say, "Fuck, no," and march right back into my office and start typing again.

This sort of defiance may or may not work for you.

I know of one author who writes in an office with the door closed. When he first started writing, as soon as he started feeling resistance, he'd stand up and yell at his critical voice, ordering them out of the room while the door was closed.

You'll have to come up with what works for you while you're writing.

One of the things that I've learned about critical voice through the years is that if left idle, your critical voice will turn its thoughts to other evil. You may think that you've beaten critical voice, only to discover that it's found a different pathway into your head while you're creating.

Instead, you need to give critical voice a job. Train it to do something else. Between telling it *fuck off* and giving it something to regularly do, I find I'm rarely bothered by critical voice anymore.

One of the ways I use critical voice is when I'm reading. (Remember, critical voice is all about art, and consuming story is a way of experiencing art.) I tell critical voice to pay attention to all that grammar so that I don't have to. Not to critique the story, no, I want to *enjoy* the story and not read it critically. All critical voice is to do is to point out anything that's grammatically interesting.

Surprised the hell out of me the first time it worked. I found myself stopping in the middle of a page with what felt like a Jack Russel Terrier bouncing up and down just out of eyesight.

Turned out to be a very interesting paragraph that was a single sentence, masterfully broken up with colons and semicolons. (It was in *The Queen's Gambit* by Walter Trevor.) It was lovely to be able to stop, examine that paragraph, figure out what exactly the writer was doing both grammatically as well as emotionally, praise critical voice for doing such a good job, then be able to continue reading and just enjoying the story.

Other jobs that people have come up with in terms of giving critical voice something to do: putting it in charge of finishing stories or deadlines (all that fear behind making you create); organizing research (though this one can be tricky, as "not enough research" is a path critical voice may use to stop you); or even very specifically proofing a manuscript (with heavy parameters, to find mistakes and not rewrite everything).

However, not listening to critical voice is only half of the equation. The other half is hearing your creative voice.

In Conclusion:

- In addition to all the other myriad voices of characters in your head, there are two others: *critical* voice and *creative* voice.
- Critical voice is trying to keep you safe. But there is no such thing as safe art. (Or rather, safe art is boring art.)
- Critical voice can be very loud.

- You can distract your critical voice by giving it specific tasks.
- It is the rare writer who can completely defeat their critical voice. Most of the rest of us have to deal with it again and again.

FOUR

Learning to Listen to Creative Voice

CREATIVE VOICE DOESN'T SOUND anything like critical voice. Critical voice is loud. It will stop you in your tracks.

Creative voice is quiet. It, too, can stop you, once you start learning to listen to it.

Critical voice says everything is wrong, this isn't any good, etc.

Creative voice, when it speaks up, may point out that something is wrong. However, creative voice generally also shows up with an answer to what's wrong. How to fix it. Critical voice *never* does that.

Creative voice is also that part of you that makes you write in a white, hot flurry. It encourages you to fly, to jump off that cliff and let your wings form as you fall. Creative voice is in a hurry once you start going.

For me, one of the most apparent places creative voice comes into play is when I'm in the middle of a project and I start to slow down. Words which had been flowing suddenly slow to a trickle. Or I can't write at all.

Critical voice is sure to show up at that point, telling me that I'm doing it all wrong. Doubt creeps in.

I have to remind myself that I know how to write. I've

done it before. I know how to tell a story. There's just something wrong in this particular place.

At that point, I close my computer and I go for a walk. Or I do dishes. Or maybe go pull some weeds. Something, anything physical.

Hopefully creative voice will get back to me sooner rather than later. But that's the other thing about creative voice. Critical voice jumps in immediately. Creative voice will take her own sweet time getting back to me. Maybe an hour later she'll speak up. Or a couple of days. (For me, the more I listen to creative voice and encourage her, the faster she shows up.)

Eventually, though, creative voice starts speaking and explains what I was doing wrong as well as how to fix it.

Again, this is a quiet voice. She isn't jumping up and down with harsh boots all over your manuscript. This is a wisp come up to tickle your side, blow gently in your ear, and give you the solution.

My husband finds creative voice while he's driving. Sometimes I'll hear creative voice then. Other people find her in the shower, that voice that tells you the next part of the story, or how to fix this broken section.

I didn't realize I was waiting for creative voice until I heard about her, and how quiet she was. Then I started looking for her. That voice was so quiet at first. I remember one of the first times she spoke up, though, while I was walking around the block after being frustrated with what I was writing.

She had the perfect, elegant solution. All I had to do was to stop and listen.

I do everything that I can to encourage creative voice. This includes not rewriting.

On Rewriting

When you rewrite, or you write a messy first draft, what you're telling creative voice is that she isn't important.

"I can fix it later." These are some of the most deadly words you can utter to creative voice. In essence, what you're telling them is that they aren't good enough. You don't ever want to treat your two year old like a two year old. They are important, and what they come up with is good enough to make it to the final draft.

It's an insidious way to kill your creative voice, but it's really effective. It puts critical voice in charge, and that's not where your heart is. It creates safe art, which isn't really art.

One of the ways I create a clean first draft is through a technique called *cycling*. This is going back over what you've written while still in creative voice, not in critical voice.

When I start a new piece, if I don't run into any problems, I'll write hard and fast until I take a break. When I return to what I'm working on, I'll start some place above where I finished, whether at the start of a scene or the start of a chapter. I'll go through it, not allowing myself to get bogged down, but just to skim it, recapture the voice and the spirit of what I was doing. I may fix things while I'm going through it. I may not. Then I'll hit the end and I'll start flowing forward again.

It's really important to pay attention to how you are feeling when you're going back through your work.

If you're dreading it, or it feels onerous to you, guess what? That's critical voice talking.

If you're excited, and you find yourself rushing through it, because you really want to get to the next part, that's creative voice at work.

It may take some time to teach yourself to cycle through your work using only creative voice. You'll have to let go of a lot of perfectionism. You'll have to start learning how to trust yourself, trust your creative voice.

But the more trust you put into your creative voice, the stronger she'll get.

Trust me.

Whenever I get back to a piece that I've already started, I'll generally begin where I started the previous day, and go through all those words before I get back to my flow. It means the first hour is frequently slower than the rest of the hours I write. Sometimes that isn't the case, and I get through that previous section in less than ten minutes and I press on. Other times, I'll spend most of an hour going through the previous section, adding what needs to be added (generally) before I start adding new words.

Often while I'm writing, I'll come upon a new fact or detail that will need to get added to an earlier section of the piece. Generally, I'll stop where I am, go to where I need to add that information, then write it. I'll clean up whatever needs cleaning, then I'll start making forward progress again.

For me, until everything is in place, I won't be able to move forward. I can no longer just leave myself a note. I get to go back and fix everything, make it all work.

Cycling is an important skill that you'll need to teach yourself. You'll need to find a balance between doing too much and too little. I know of a writer who only writes short stories because when he cycles, he always starts at the beginning of the story. That generally only works at the beginning, especially as you start writing longer pieces. This is why I usually start with the words I wrote the previous day. As I tend to write between 3-5000 words a day, this isn't too much to go through.

There are times when I'm doing a writing marathon, and I'll write 10,000 words per day. I'll do small bits of cycling during such a project, just going back to the previous section when I start writing after a break. I won't go over everything more than once, though. I don't have time if I'm going to get that many words done in a day.

However, one of the things about writing so rapidly is that it tends to be cleaner than a usual writing session. I'll enter what's called "flow state" when I make fewer mistakes. They've actually done studies on it, where in laboratory tests, writers, painters, or musicians demonstrate that they make fewer errors once they enter flow state.

Getting into flow state on a regular basis is something else that helps creative voice. It allows her to be free and encourages her to be present for longer periods of time.

This is again one of those things that you'll only get better at with practice. Hopefully your creative voice will start talking with you sooner rather than later.

In Conclusion:

- Creative voice is what makes writing fun.
- Creative voice tends to be much quieter than critical voice. Instead of just pointing out what's wrong, creative voice tends to show up with solutions.
- Learning how to cycle through your writing using creative voice will help you achieve a clean first draft. The difference between cycling and rewriting is all in how you feel.

FIVE

The Giggle Test (Writing is Hard!)

Writing is *important*.

Writing is *hard work*.

Writing fast is bad. Having fun while you're writing, well, it can't be any good, can it? It must be a struggle.

All of that is bullshit, by the way. Particularly if you're thinking about a long-term writing career.

Once you start telling yourself that your writing is *important*, you're letting critical voice in. You'll start to slow down, or be afraid to write because the current story you want to tell isn't important enough.

Writing is *not* hard work. Sitting or standing at a computer while making shit up isn't difficult. Smoothing out poured concrete is difficult. Laying down a tile floor using large tiles is difficult. Digging a trench that's three feet deep and seventy feet long is difficult. (And yes, I've done all of the above. Life in the country.)

Writing is *not* difficult.

If you are struggling with your writing, if the words are not flowing, if it's hard, that's generally a sign that something is wrong and you need to fix that before you can move on.

For me, there are several things I have to consider if I start thinking that the writing is hard that morning.

I had surgery a few months ago, and the writing has been difficult since then, though it's growing a lot more easy. Part of it was just being out of practice writing. Part of it was that physically, I wasn't in any shape to write. My body still hurt too much and too much of my energy was being taken up with the healing process. Plus, it took a while for me to get over the opioids. I was never addicted. They just made my brain fuzzy and it took longer than I had expected to get them all washed out of my system.

So if I'm having difficulty writing some morning, I have to look at the physical side of things. Did I get enough sleep? I do not consume caffeine on a habitual basis, just every once in a while, medicinally. Do I need caffeine that morning? Is there some other chemical imbalance that I need to address?

Sometimes, there are extra issues in your world that are making the writing difficult, such as a sick spouse, the death of a beloved pet, and so on. Do you need to make more space for yourself, and be gentle with yourself, rather than writing at this time? Be honest. Writing may help you get over what you're dealing with. It may not.

Before the pandemic, I would regularly go and write at coffee shops. I can't do that at this time. However, I'm lucky enough that I have more than one location at the property that I can go and write at. Do you need to go and write someplace else this writing session? Get a different perspective by writing in a different place? Move from your office to the couch? Or from the kitchen table to your bedroom?

As I mentioned before, I pay attention when the words slow down. Generally it means that I've done something wrong above where I'm currently at in the manuscript. Do I need to go fix something before I can move on? More than once, I've had to toss out the last few paragraphs of work and start over because I took a wrong turn and my subconscious noticed it first.

That happened recently in a short story I was writing. For the most part, the short story was *very* weird. Then I took a turn for the mundane. Had to throw out that entire scene and start over.

Another thing I have to look at if the writing starts to grow more difficult—where am I looking? I tend to write into the dark, with no idea of where I'm going. Am I paying attention to where I am, where the character is and what he or she is doing? Or has critical voice snuck in and said something like, "You don't know where you're going! You have to figure that out!"

Which I don't. No, really. I don't. Looking out, away from the page, is stopping me. I need to focus on what's immediately in front of me if I want to continue. I have to trust creative voice, that she knows what she's doing. The solution will be there when I arrive there. I don't have to figure it out ahead of time.

But these are all things to do after the writing starts. One of the ways that I make sure that the writing stays fun before I start a new project is what I call The Giggle Test™.

Like most writers, I always have more than one project I could write on at any point. How do I choose which one at any given time?

My process is to think about each one of those projects, one at a time, and watch my reaction to them as I consider each.

Which project makes me giggle most? Which one am I most excited about? Which one is going to drag me to the computer, demanding that I write more about it? It's always, *always* easier to write a project that you like, as opposed to one that you think you should.

You're an artist. Who has an unruly two-year-old calling the shots. There is no *should*.

What would you write about if you had no constraints? What would make you giggle? Or laugh maniacally if there's a high body count? (I've chosen projects based on both.) What is going to bring you joy?

I don't care if you *shouldn't* write that. I don't care what other people are going to think. I don't care if it isn't trendy or marketable.

Remember, if you can see the bandwagon, it's already too late to join. Instead, cut your own trail. Trust that people will follow you. You will be someone's favorite writer.

Learn how to giggle while you're writing. This takes practice, but you also need to pick the correct projects. The more you enjoy yourself, the more your readers will enjoy your writing.

One of the things you may need to do in order to make the writing more fun is to reframe how you talk about it.

When I first started off, I needed to change my language. Instead of saying, "I have to write" or "It's now my writing time, so go write" I would say, "I get to go write now" or "Yay! Writing time!"

That change in attitude helped me remember the fun of what I was doing. And writing is fun.

One of the reasons why the myth of *writing is hard* is so difficult to shake is because it isn't just you who believes this. This myth is far spread, and begins when you're in school. Teachers deliberately slow students down. They don't want you to write too much, or too fast. They can't keep up with you.

So they tell you at an early age that writing is hard. Since they're in a position of authority, and you're young, you might tend to believe them. Even if you know personally that writing is easy. You'll instead start to think that you're doing it wrong.

In addition, as a reader, you might want to believe that writing is hard because if an artist has worked really hard on this piece, it has more value. Something that's quick and easy can't possibly have value, at least not to a reader.

Therefore, most writers, particularly full time commercial artists, lie about how hard they work, how much they struggle. They're actually having fun. But in our society, fun isn't work. Fun isn't something that's worth money. Fun isn't important.

Yet as a writer, fun is one of the most important aspects of your work. Though fun isn't always the right word.

You're an entertainer. Your work should be enjoyable. It might also teach things, slyly, if you're doing it right. Again, this is for commercial artists, not literary ones.

So have fun while you're writing. Making it a struggle is a sure fire way to reach burnout.

Remember, you don't have to tell other people how much fun you're having, or how easy a piece was to write. Keep that to yourself, and just let your two-year-old play.

In Conclusion:

- Making the writing *important* allows critical voice to take control and stop you from writing.
- Choose writing projects based on whether or not they'll delight *you*, not anyone else.
- Pay attention to the language you use when talking about your writing. Don't refer to it as a chore, but as a reward and something you're looking forward to doing.
- Writing is not hard. Or difficult. It's supposed to be fun and easy. Pay attention to how you're feeling as you're writing. If it starts to get difficult, critical voice has stepped in.

SIX

Ideas are Cheap

I KNOW, I know. How can ideas possibly be cheap? I mean, the subscription to the service "IdeasRUs" costs thousands of dollars every month!

Right?

Beginning writers ask, "Where do you get your ideas?" This puts writers in the mindset that ideas are precious, that they're hard work.

I sort of believed in this myth when I started. Not too much, but a little. I bought myself fancy notebooks in which to keep track of my ideas, writing them all down so that they wouldn't scurry off and I'd lose track of them. (I honestly was more excited about owning all those fancy notebooks than actually writing in any of them.)

Except that I always lost track of those ideas anyway. I rarely went back to those notebooks. I was always coming up with something new, and frequently, fresher. I eventually stopped writing the ideas down, because even when I did go back to those notebooks, I'd never use anything I'd written there.

When I was searching around for a story idea, I always found that a better place to start than those old moldy notebooks was to ask myself, "What topic am I most interested in right now?"

The answer to that question was frequently very enlightening, and a much better idea was sure to come from that, something that I'd like writing, that would make me giggle a lot while I was writing.

For example, the entire Seattle Trolls trilogy came into being one morning because I had the book I was "supposed" to write, and had no interest in writing, and a lot of time on my hands. (I was currently on a writing retreat and I was expecting to write a lot that weekend.)

The answer to the question was, "Transformations." That was the general topic that I was really thinking a lot about in the back of my head.

The entire first novel (*The Changeling Troll*) came about because of that one answer. Followed by five more books.

I have been gently scolded by other writers for *not* treating my ideas as if they were pure gold, that is, valuable but at the same time, malleable.

I call bullshit.

By telling my creative voice that ideas are cheap and easy, she is constantly throwing new ones my way. If I was treating each and every idea as precious, she wouldn't come up with as many. All the damned time.

(Experienced writers don't ask where ideas come from. They ask, "How do you make them stop coming?" I have SO MANY more ideas than I have time to write.)

Aren't I afraid that I'll lose one? That I won't remember a really good one? Don't I have regrets?

When I started writing? Yes. I had regrets about those things that had to be better than what I was currently doing. Until I learned to trust myself, trust that I was always going to have more and better ideas. And my creative voice learned that she was free to whisper all those ideas in my ear, at all times.

I will regularly think about whatever project I'm working on late at night, as I'm going to sleep. That way, writer brain can think about the story while I'm sleeping. Frequently, if I've been stuck about something in the novel, my creative voice will have a solution by the time I wake up.

The very few times that I've bothered to actually write down the ideas I've come up with at night, I've found that I'm disappointed in the morning when I transfer whatever is on my phone to my computer.

The idea may be good. But if I don't write it down, don't freeze it on the page, if I give writer brain a chance to mull over whatever it is and expand on it, chances are, in the morning, whatever I thought of the night before will be gone and something so much better will be in its place.

Every once in a while I will write something down late at night. And it isn't because I'm afraid I'll lose whatever inspiration it is that I've had. It's because it's the start of a story, and if I don't write it down, writer brain is going to obsess over that idea, those words, all night long and I'll never get to sleep. Sometimes what I've written down on my phone at night is golden. It's exactly what I need to start whatever it is.

Other times, it's pure drivel and I end up deleting it. Or trying to use it, and then spending hours going over it until I've redrafted the entire thing anyway.

One of the exercises that I was given at a novel plotting workshop was to think of an idea for a particular novel.

Then throw it away.

Think of a second idea.

Throw it away.

Think of a third idea.

You guessed it. Throw that one away too.

By the time you get to your fourth idea, you're probably going to be onto something unique. No clichés by that point. You might be writing a really special novel once you go through this.

The first time I heard of this method, I thought it was a bunch of hooey. Who would go through that sort of process? Wasn't that just making all the writing harder when it's supposed to be fun and easy? And wouldn't this punish creative voice by telling her that her ideas weren't any good?

Then I tried to consciously do it, only to realize that I was unconsciously doing it with every single story I told. I was always going through the "nope, too obvious, too clichéd, too boring," thought process for the first three or four ideas until I landed on the right idea, which was generally number four or five. I've since learned that even some of those first ideas can be made unique and memorable because I'm telling them from my point of view, with my voice, which no one else has.

But again, this means that I'm always coming up with ideas. They're always flowing out. The really good ones stick.

In Conclusion:

- Ideas aren't precious commodities. They're cheap and easy. And they come by the dozen.
- Holding onto old ideas may make your writing stale. Instead, write something you're passionate about.
- Try throwing out your original ideas when you start a project, so that you might come up with something unique and truly you.

SEVEN

Gaining Speed

I will admit, I'm a bit frustrated with my own writing speed at this time. As I said, I'm still recovering from major surgery.

My normal pace is between 1200-1500 words per hour. At this point, I'm barely managing 1000 words per hour. More like 800 most hours. Particularly for the first writing session of any longer block.

Normally, I write for three to four hours every morning, broken up into one hour sessions. I used to be able to regularly write 3000 words in three hours, with breaks every hour. Now, it takes me four hours to do that same amount of work. I need more and longer breaks than I used to, again, because I'm still healing.

I'm hoping that eventually I'll get my speed back. We'll see.

But how did I achieve such speeds in the first place?

Remember, I started out writing everything out by hand, first, then moving to typing on the computer. So it took twice as long at first to write everything.

Typing out on the computer I believe I started around 500 words per hour. Maybe. I just remember it took a lot of hours and there had to be a better, faster way to write.

Then I found Rachel Aaron/ Rachel Bach, and her post about how she went from writing 2000 words a day to 10,000.

http://thisblogisaploy.blogspot.com/2011/06/how-i-went-from-writing-2000-words-day.html

She's even written a book on it. *2K to 10K, Writing Faster, Writing Better, and Writing More of What You Love.*

Her primary points are as follows:

- What *time* of day to you write best?
- What are you writing about *now*?
- What makes you *excited* about your writing?

I already knew that I wrote best in the early mornings, though I figured out that my second best time was in the evenings, just after dinner.

I started off each writing session by jotting down a few notes about what I was about to write about. I didn't have to plan everything out. I just had to figure out the immediate next section. I learned how to just do a little planning, and only think about the amount of story that I could write in that writing session.

I also regained my enthusiasm for the project during those writing sessions. As I jotted down notes (still writing by hand) I would think about all the cool stuff I was going to get to write. As I wrote up my few notes, I'd grow more and more excited until I was brimming with enthusiasm and would hop over to the computer and go like mad.

Eventually, I figured out how to get there without writing down notes ahead of time. I could just start at the computer and my fingers would be flying.

There have been times, like now, when I've had to relearn my speed. What am I currently doing to help with that?

One of the things that I've done in the past has been timed writing sprints. If you want to look it up, it's called the Pomodoro method. Basically, you start with a small amount of time, say, fifteen to twenty minutes. You get an actual timer, something that either sits on your desk or a timer that runs on your computer.

Start the timer, and start to write. There is no rewriting, no cycling during this writing time. This is all about speed. Don't stop to edit. Don't stop to correct spelled words or misused grammar. Just write, as much as you can, as fast as you can.

Then, once the alarm goes off, stop. You may end up stopping mid-sentence or mid-paragraph. (I do tend to finish the word I was typing, but that's it.)

Now, take a break. This part is as equally important as doing the sprint. Step away from the computer. Go stretch out your hands and arms. Take a walk around the block. Some people set a second timer and allow themselves ten minutes on social media or checking email. I can't do that. That takes me too far out of the zone.

After you take your break, and the break should also be timed, start your next writing session.

When you're first starting, don't do too many sessions in a row. Two or three at most. Keep them short and focused. You're training yourself to write without stopping. You'll be tired at first. This is a muscle that you're building.

But what about the cycling and rewriting? That comes later, after you've trained yourself to write when you get to your computer. If you feel confident that every time you sit down, you'll start writing, then you can start with a cycle first.

Play around with the amount of time that makes a good writing session for you. I do forty-five to fifty minutes, then I take a ten to fifteen minute break. I have a friend who does ninety minute sessions, but then takes a thirty minute break. I know of another writer who does twenty-five minutes, with a five minute break. We're all different, with different amounts of focus time.

At this point, I don't use a timer on my computer. Instead, I have my Tyrant of Movement, AKA my Fitbit. It tells me at ten minutes before the hour that I need to get up and walk 250 steps. That way, I get in my steps every day, as well as my words.

Another thing for increasing speed: do your research ahead of time.

Research time is *not* writing time. They are two different things. Find some other time to do your research. Do it in the evenings, or set aside some of your regular writing time to do research. Do not try to conflate the two.

When I write historic pieces, I generally do all the research ahead of time, before I start writing a word. Either that, or I know a time period well enough that I can get most of the details correct without doing any additional research.

There are times, though, when I come upon something that I really need to look up.

One of the ways I increased my speed was I got myself a dedicated writing computer. It doesn't have to be an expensive machine. The only programs running on it are Word and Excel. I don't have any games on that machine. I also don't have any internet access.

When I stumble into something that I need to know right then, as I'm writing, and I think it's something I can quickly look up, I allow myself to look it up on my phone.

It annoys me to read things on my phone. I keep the settings that way on purpose. So that I'll look up what I need, then get back to the writing. It's much more difficult to get lost, going down a TV-tropes rabbit hole on my phone because I purposefully make it not easy.

If it really is a big thing and I can't get to it on my phone, I use brackets around the piece so that I can go and do research at another point and get back to the story. This only works sometimes for me. If it's that important of a detail, chances are I'm going to need to move to my other computer, the one that is connected to the internet, and spend some time finding what I need. It means ending a writing session early.

One of the other things that helps writers gain speed is what has been referred to as "ground effect." Basically, it means that if you're writing enough words every day, the writing becomes easier as you practice and do it. "Enough words" is different for every writer. For me, it needs to be between one to two thousand every day before ground effect kicks in and the writing becomes closer to effortless. For others, I've heard as low as two hundred and fifty words per day, and as high as three thousand. It really depends on the writer. (This isn't the same as learning to write every day. You're looking for speed, not accountability. If all you're focused on is writing every day, I know writers who focus on just getting at least one or two sentences per day.)

It's practice. It's getting to the page, day after day. It's spending the time writing, not rewriting, not editing, not researching, but actually writing. Doing this repeatedly will speed up your writing.

In Conclusion:

- Speed is something you can learn. And yes, you can learn to write quickly without sacrificing quality.
- Timed writing sprints may help you gain speed. This is all about the writing, though. You'll have to cycle back through the draft at another time.
- Ground effect is when you write enough every day that the writing gets easier. The amount you may need to write to achieve this may differ from other writers.

EIGHT

Beyond Book One

FOR THE LONGEST TIME, I could only write the first book in any series. I *knew* that there were additional books about those characters that I could write.

I had no clue how to go about writing them, however.

This was partly a case of new!shiny! syndrome. Every new idea was so exciting, so captivating. I never wanted to go back and revisit something *old*. That would be *boring*.

So for a lot of years, I had single books. Many single books. I had tried unsuccessfully to start the second book for some of those series. However, I couldn't engage my writer brain. She was just uninterested in continuing on. She'd *finished* that book. There was nothing more to say.

I'd asked other writers who wrote multiple books in a series how they did it. Unfortunately, the advice they gave was completely wrong for me. They said it was like visiting old friends, getting together and hanging out.

Ugh.

Not what I wanted to do. Sure, I like visiting old friends. But writing is more of an exciting thing for me. It's jumping off that cliff and letting my wings form on the way down.

Finally, I asked another writer, who also suffered from the

new!shiny! syndrome. (Also known as popcorn kittens, every time you think they've settled down, yet another one jumps up. https://www.youtube.com/watch?v=JDABjGGeZzM)

She told me that the way she engages her brain is to make every novel *different*. Sure, the same characters, but give them a new problem. New villains. And also introduce new characters.

Ding! Ding! Ding! Ding!

That was what I needed to hear.

In my opinion, I don't believe that some of my initial second books were as successful as they could have been. I took "make it different" to an extreme. (Though a writer is always the worst judge of her work. I know that for some people, those second and third novels are their favorites of mine.)

My husband almost always writes in series. That's how he thinks. One of the reasons for our differences was how we read as children.

He read comic books, which are always serialized stories. I read either single books or trilogies. I didn't necessarily read long series. When I look back, I realize that I would grow bored with all the books set in the same world.

He is the one who gave me the concept of extended universe. (He wrote a Business for Breakfast book about it: *Series and Continuity for Professional Writers* https://www.knottedroadpress.com/book/series-and-continuity-for-professional-writers/.) For those of you familiar with the Marvel Universe movies, it's the same idea. All those characters have their own stories and their own lives, but occasionally they also intersect.

Romance does this particularly successfully, with the main characters in novel one getting their happily ever after, followed by telling the best friend's story, then their cousin's story, or maybe the story of the other person they work with. Some have a very specific setting, then everyone in that setting gets a book, like a medical romance series, where every doctor in the hospital finally finds their one true love.

Again, that's visiting old friends. That still does not appeal to me.

Instead, I continue the story, generally with the characters I started with.

This gets me to the idea of a trilogy. A trilogy can follow a three-act structure, writ large. Each book may or may not have a complete resolution. Sometimes there will be a cliffhanger at the end of each book. Other times, book one will be complete, while books two and three will be more of a duology.

Remember, with the three-act structure, the rough shorthand goes like this: Hero, Villain, Victory.

The first book is pretty easy. You're writing about your hero.

The second book is where it might get more tricky. It's part of the reason why people sometimes call the middle of their book the mushy middle. They need to focus on the villain, and being conflict avoidant, they feel uncomfortable doing that. Plus, if they're like me, they don't start out wanting to make their main character suffer that much. They pull their punches.

I eventually learned that it was okay for me to torture my characters. Most readers want to read about characters growing. It's boring if everything's too easy. I don't write horror, so it's all right if my characters have some difficulty. (When I wasn't in a safe place personally, I found myself doing more vague outlining for my novels than usual, just to reassure myself that everything was going to be okay eventually.)

Villains can be fun. They can also be disturbing when you think about all that nastiness that was just waiting inside of you. I think of it as cathartic. The reason why I'm not an ax murderess is because I can kill people in my novels. There is more than one character who ends up badly who is very loosely based on someone who's recently pissed me off.

So focus on your hero, but be sure to not forget your villain. You can lean on them to move your novel along. After all, they still consider themselves to be the hero, right?

The third novel, then, is all about victory, but it starts in the darkest place. That can also be a challenge. Let yourself go there, and trust yourself that you can bring some light out of this dreaded black night.

There are ways of subverting this. Instead of writing a trilogy, you write a series, almost a monster of the week sort of thing. It isn't the same problems, however. It's always different problems, with different solutions.

Now, I regularly write books that are both standalone, as well as both trilogies and series. I will admit that I'm much more comfortable with trilogies. I read a lot of fantasy trilogies when I was a kid, so it's something that I can easily fall back on.

So if you're having problems with only writing a single book, think back on what you read as a child, and decide where you can expand from there.

In Conclusion:

- There are ways to write past the first book, coming up with different stories.
- Be sure to focus not just on the hero, but on the villain, so you won't have a mushy middle or a horrendously difficult second novel when it comes to the writing.
- You can write an extended universe set of books instead of a trilogy or series. No one is insisting that you must do one or the other. Write what brings you joy.

NINE

No Secret Handshake

IN MY LATE TWENTIES, I got really lucky and found an amazing writing group.

I understand now just how lucky I was. Many, if not most, writing groups are toxic. (Or they start out well enough, and get awful quickly.) They focus on critique instead of writing. There are people there who take delight in tearing other people's writing apart. They feel as though they aren't contributing unless they offer a criticism of the author's work, a way in which someone can fix something.

There were two incredibly important concepts that this writing group imparted to me.

The first was the distinction between the writer and the work, or as they called it, the chairmaker and the chair.

We were there to discuss the *chair*, not the *chairmaker*. Everything was about the work and not the person who had done it. There was a very clear distinction between the two that the group rigidly maintained. It was a safe place to bring your writing to, no matter how personal. No one would dissect the writer or talk about them. It was always all about the work.

The other concept that they instilled in me was that no

one would ever achieve the perfect setup in order to write. Having this marvel of ergonomics for a chair wasn't going to get you to the page. Same with the perfect desk, or even the best pen in the world.

There had to be something else that got you to the page. You could always improve your writing setup. And it didn't matter.

What mattered was the writing.

A writer writes. Period.

Because I learned this so early in my writing career, it was easy to understand, then, that a single trick with your writing wouldn't bring you success, however you defined it.

Learning this one technique for making believable characters isn't going to make you an instant bestseller. Same with finally understanding all the emotional beats in your story, hammering those out until it's a masterpiece of an emotional rollercoaster.

Nope.

The shorthand that we've come up with is, *There is no secret handshake.*

If this editor would just buy my work, I'll be rich!

If I learn how to successfully do these ads, all my books will suddenly start selling!

If I spend thousands of dollars on that consultant, all my woes will be solved!

It doesn't work that way.

First of all, as we have learned over the years, my husband and I don't make our living from a single book. We have a very large catalogue, over 400 titles at this point. Some of those books don't sell. Others sell a few copies here and there. Still others sell many copies on a regular basis.

But even those books that sell well aren't enough to make a living from.

Instead, it's everything, all together. Those drops—a nickel here and there—add up into a rather nice cash stream.

And how did we get here?

Time. Practice. Butt in chair, fingers on keyboard. Taking risks now and again. Following our heart when it comes to writing, our passion.

Do we write to market? Not really. Writing to market is yet another secret handshake. IF you love that market, and IF you understand and can incorporate all the genre tropes for that market, and IF you're lucky, then it might work.

Might.

But if you don't love that market, you will burn out. I've seen it.

Even if you love that market, you might eventually burn out anyway.

One of the saddest things I've ever listened to was a podcast by a person who wrote well when he wrote from his heart. But he'd started believing that he needed to outline his work, that it must have certain emotional story beats.

And now, he couldn't write anymore.

But he didn't realize that putting that sort of structure on his writing, instead of letting it flow, was what was killing his ability to write. In the podcast, he was blaming everything else. I stopped listening to that podcast after that. It was too heartbreaking.

Because he believed in that secret handshake, and not in his own work.

And even if you get everything right, that book still may not sell.

Even if you think you got everything wrong, a book might surprise you and take off into the stratosphere.

How do you know?

You don't.

And that's the main illusion that the secret handshake gives you. That you, as an artist, might have control over your work, over what sells and what doesn't.

Do ads work? Sometimes. Anyone who's worked in advertising will tell you that 50% of all ads work. They just never know which half.

Are there things you can do to ensure that your work sells better than it has been?

Possibly.

Make sure that your passive marketing is in place. The metadata. The cover. The blurb. The sample.

Then write the next book.

If there is a secret handshake, it's that. Writing more will bring you more discoverability, more ways for your audience to find you, more avenues to sell.

But honestly, there really isn't a single secret handshake that will bring you success.

And learning that might be the most important thing you can do in terms of your career.

In Conclusion:

- There is no secret handshake, no one thing that will bring you success.
- For us, as well as most of the writers I know, it isn't a single book either. It's having a catalogue, with many different books, that will bring you success.
- There is no secret handshake.

Afterword

So here ends this account of my writing journey, how I went from believing in all the traditional myths to becoming a happy, successful, productive, independent writer.

As I said in the introduction, your path may not follow the same lines. In fact, I can practically guarantee that your path will be different. Think of my journey as a series of signposts leading toward the big mountain in the distance.

You may decide to stop at some of the same roadside attractions that I've listed. Or they may not be that interesting to you. You will absolutely have a different perspective on what I've listed here.

The most important thing to realize, though, is that this is a journey. You don't have to stay where you are, particularly if the writing isn't bringing you joy. There are other places to go, other sights to see, other roads to travel.

And that, more than anything else, is what I hope this book brings you, the impetus to start exploring, to find your own path to the mountain.

I hope to see you on the road!

About the Author

Leah Cutter tells page-turning, wildly creative stories that always leave you guessing in the middle, but completely satisfied by the end.

She writes mystery of all sorts. Her Lake Hope cozy mysteries have been well received by readers, who just want to curl up and have tea with the main character. Her Halley Brown series, revolving around a private investigator who used to be with the Seattle Police Department, leave you guessing at every turn. And her speculative mysteries, such as the Alvin Goodfellow Case Files—a 1930s PI set on the moon—have garnered great reviews.

She's been published in magazines such as *Alfred Hitchcock's Mystery Magazine* and in anthologies like *Fiction River: Spies*. On top of that, Leah is the editor of the new quarterly mystery magazine: *Mystery, Crime, and Mayhem*.

Find Leah's books on Knotted Road Press at www.KnottedRoadPress.com

Follow her blog at www.LeahCutter.com.

Read more mysteries at www.MysteryCrimeAndMayhem.com.

Reviews

It's true. Reviews help me sell more books. If you've enjoyed this story, please consider leaving a review of it on your favorite site.

Come someplace new…

Are you a traveler? Do you enjoy exploring strange new worlds, new cultures, new people?

Journey into the various lands envisioned by Leah Cutter.

Sign up for my newsletter and I'll start you on your travels with a free copy of my book, *The Island Sampler*.

I will never spam you or use your email for nefarious purposes. You can also unsubscribe at any time.

http://www.LeahCutter.com/newsletter/

About Knotted Road Press

Knotted Road Press fiction specializes in dynamic writing set in mysterious, exotic locations.

Knotted Road Press non-fiction publishes autobiographies, business books, cookbooks, and how-to books with unique voices.

Knotted Road Press creates DRM-free ebooks as well as high-quality print books for readers around the world.

With authors in a variety of genres including literary, poetry, mystery, fantasy, and science fiction, Knotted Road Press has something for everyone.

Knotted Road Press
www.KnottedRoadPress.com

www.ingramcontent.com/pod-product-compliance
Lightning Source LLC
Chambersburg PA
CBHW071124030426
42336CB00013BA/2203